REVERIE

Major Ashes

To the sun

Acknowledgments

I feel overwhelmed with gratitude and love for all the people who helped me when I was at my lowest. There were a lot. I was a menace and it took a village.

I think I put Kat, Alicia, and my mom through the most hell though. So I think I owe them the biggest thank you. Seriously, thank you.

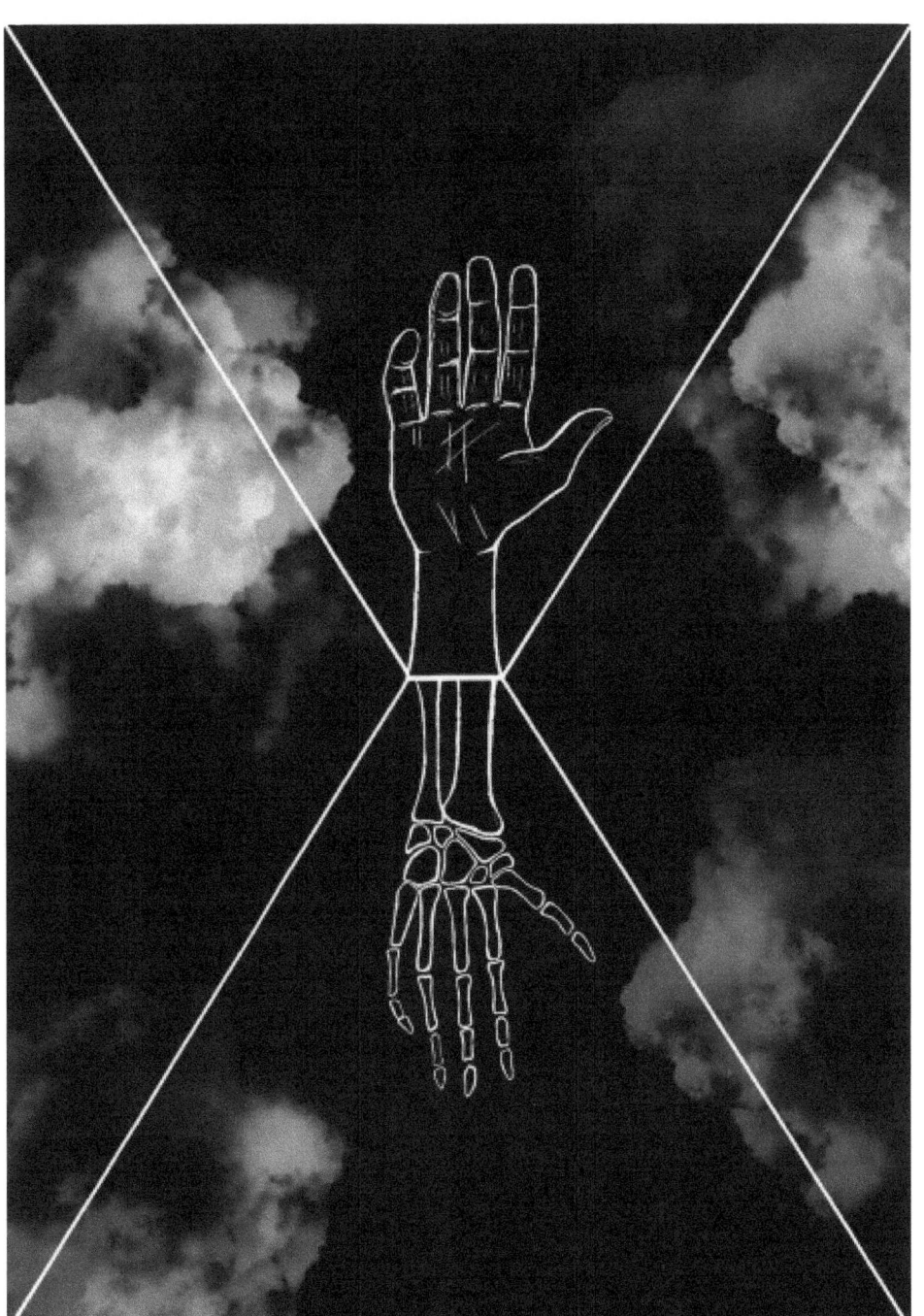

Reflection

It's all over.
All of it has passed me by.
I'm so afraid if I let go, I'll lose the warmth,
I'll lose the time.
But the time is lost.
The warmth is gone.
I'm a skeleton with sand in her palm.

Running through foreign land, this is what I wanted, is it not?
To be alone.
Is that not why I was so cold?

I kept running towards something I couldn't name.
In this mirror I look her in the face.
Scared of my reflection, I don't meet her eyes.
She's desperate to go back in time.
I keep trying to make bribes, all of them denied.

But if I write it all down, history will keep it safe.
That's the best I can give to my sweet heartbreak.
To love I've recklessly thrown away.
Please don't let it go to waste.

THE DREAMER

The Dreamer

Woe is me.
Lost in fantasy.
Can't face reality.

I'm the dreamer.
I follow a trend.
I'm obsessed with controlling the end.

I keep reaching for clouds I have no intention to hold.
Real love is fool's gold.
I feel bad for the hearts I've kept close.
Most of all, my own.

Cheers to the hearts that think love's real.
Cheers to mine, whom I've never let heal.
Let's pretend I'm human until the story gets old.
My desperate skeleton is cold.

Misery Loves Company

Who has risked it all for me?
Who would even try?
Am I worth the leap?
Or am I someone you sneak in at night?
I've been loved, but have I ever been liked?

Oh, to be in someone's day dream.
Romanticized an entire life.
Have I caught someone's eye?
Is it love at first sight?
Or am I the dandelion in a field of damsel's delights?

We're not dancing in the moonlight.
No one is singing outside my window.
No one is making sure I get home alright.
We're not kissing in the rain.
Maybe I am cursed to only be loved by pain.

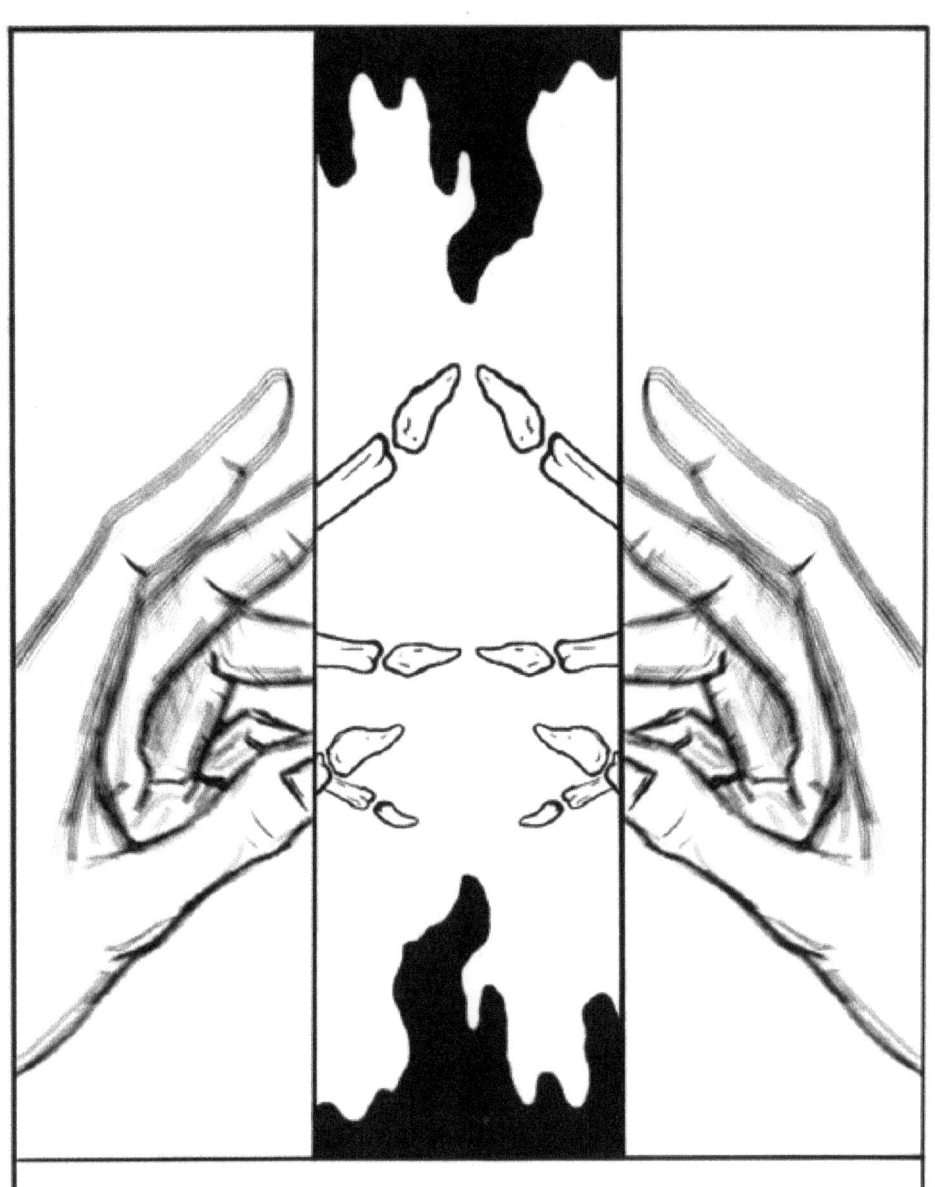

WINTER

Northern Lights

You spoil me with treasures and gifts.
Nothing withheld.
Servitude, you do best.

To taste magic,
An ethereal body shake.
I know I'll regret this
But with true love, chances you take.

Dance with me.
We're the only ones in the room.
Like the ocean and the moon, you influence my every move.
Snowflakes on my tongue,
Lilies in your hair,
Midnight movies,
And twitterpated stares.

In your eyes,
I see the northern lights.
And in mine,
You see the sunrise.

Afterlife

Winter
Winter
Winter

I almost wonder if I've been brainwashed
Into believing you're the one.
Since I'm not sure even death would be enough.

When I die, I'll wake to see your eyes.
I'd recognize you in any life.
I can give no hello
And there is no goodbye.
I think we'll meet in the afterlife.

Winter

Your love is harsh.
Your beauty, striking.
White flames, enticing.
You have the eyes of a dreamer.
They remind me of my own.
You remind me of winter:
A stark, desperate cold.

Snow over the ocean, northern skies
Ice-cold secrets, seductive prize.
I love how the moon shines at night.
Even the frost is mesmerized.

Soul's unique like each snowflake,
But our two souls are one and the same.
Never have I ever felt a cold flame.
I thought I knew what music was, until you said my name.

Frozen together we've stopped time.
Are you even real?
Or just in my mind?
A fantasy?
A tragedy?
That ends with death?
For you, I would give my very last breath.

Tear open my skin.
Let the bitter air in.
Bone-crushing secrets.
Liars never win.
I'll go to hell for my insolent sin.

WINTER

So, I won't ask God to let us in.
That's not where we're going.
I'll be surprised if they ever let us leave purgatory.
How many times now have I disappointed the all-knowing?
My scarlet A is showing.

Buried in snow
Yet, our memories refuse to erode.
I abandoned my religion only for you to turn me to stone.

You have the eyes of a sinner.
They remind me of my own.
You remind me of winter:
A stark, desperate cold.

Frostbite

I was a tender age.
You were past your prime.
But we danced in the attic
Where I committed my crime.

The swan became a crow.
What does Benvolio know?
Forbidden love is fire to some,
Even with the risk of a crimson glow.

But I was cautious of the flames.
I thought I was being brave.
Where is the fire?
It's the middle of winter.
Hell froze over!

I thought I was clever.
Until I saw my reflection in the ice,
I was covered in frostbite.
We burned so hot it was cold.
In my delusion, I didn't know.
Children get distracted by snow.

In winter, ripe fruit is hard to find.
I guess that's why you left nothing but the rind.
You devoured my light.
Was the hunt worth the kill? Was the fruit as sweet
Even after the tree died?
I didn't even put up a fight.
I thought I deserved to be left out to dry.

NOTHING BUT

THE RIND

The Ocean and The Moon

Forbidden appetence,
Boundaries hushed.
A moon-glade touch
Tempting ocean lust.

He influences her every move.
She admires his curves and his grooves.
He begs for a drop.
Mystified by the moon
How could she ask him to stop?

The powers of the sea
Send pieces to space.
The way she lets herself break
Just to give him a taste.

What a waste.
If you're going to burn,
If you're going to starve,
Why not do it for more
Than something as simple
As the affection of a man's heart.

Uses her talent to cry with the moon
When she could be laughing with the stars.

Gray clouds creeping,
Thunder off the coast.
He polluted her.
The one she loved most.
Trusted him with her body,

WINTER

Trusted him with her heart.
Trusted that once he saw blood,
He'd stop tearing her apart.

The sea curses the moon,
"Fall to prove loyalty!
Or at least meet me halfway."
a whisper, she begs.
But his dark side's on display.

A silent response as the sun burns her face.
And the moon hides away.
Leaving an ocean storm to rage.

Blood on your hands

With tears in my eyes and blood on my hands
I told you I couldn't do this anymore.
You said just a little while longer.
That's when I knew you didn't love me.
And if I couldn't be loved by the likes of you,
How was I to believe I'd ever be loved by someone I actually respected?

Oil in the Sea

"You don't understand;
I am just a kid."

A whisper, my heart sings.
As I contemplate my ending.
Blood on my hands is all I can see.

Mud on my face,
I reek of scum.
Like oil in the sea.

I desperately try to think
Of something dirtier than me.
Dead fish left out for days,
I wince at my selfish ways.
Burns my eyes to think about my lies.
Grind a skunk and season with dead flies.

Even roaches have a purpose.
Rats have beauty
And landfills have style.
How could I be so vile?

To betray a lover is one thing.
But to betray a friend,
It is something else entirely.

If I went to sleep
Maybe my debt would be paid.

I think I should instead suffer
For the rest of my days.
However, I've always been a runner.

WINTER

So tonight, I plunder,
Drown in the sea,
An empty bottle of pills next to me.

Who's the bigger coward?
You or me?

THE RUNNER

Alcoholic

You show up in my dreams more than I care to admit.

My subconscious holds onto you.
Like an alcoholic clutching a bottle of scotch.
I did the twelve steps
Yet, you still fester.
Even after a decade of being sober.

Why do I still think of you?
I know it's not as good as I remember.
I'm summer stuck in December.

Recovery doesn't mean to forget.
Use my liver and heart as evidence.
A truth I desperately try to suppress.

But I guess that's what happens when you ignore a mess.

It doesn't go away.
It seeps through the floors
Lingers through closed doors.
A smell you can't escape.
Dump the bleach down the drain.
Nothing can remove the stain.
A tremor in my hand that I can't shake.

We haven't spoken in years,
A habit I do not intend to break.
But I know you dream of me, too.
I know you do.

Past Life

When I faced my fears, I thought of you.
You, who used to be the color to my hue.
The moon to my ocean.
The keeper of my devotion.

It took me five years to listen to Lana Del Rey.
I go back and forth between flames of passion
And flames of pain.
You're my Genesis.
You're my stake.
You're the beginning of this hurricane.
You're my guilt.
A ripple in the lake.
A goddamn earthquake.

The night we threw snowballs,
You held me so tightly.
Kissed me with your whole body.
Like it was the end of the world.
Like it was the last time we'd meet.
That's how you treated me every time you saw me.
Our noses were red,
Our cheeks flushed.
Our hearts raced with a burning lust.
I saw fire in your eyes.
I made you feel alive.
You were my first home.
You were a piece of my soul.
You were everything I wanted.

WINTER

I thought our love was carved into stone,
A tattoo on bone.

But you were the devil knocking at my door.
You were the doctor and the knife.
You were the poison and the cure.
You brought me to the darkest parts of heaven
And to the coldest parts of hell.
You were the best.
And you were the worst.

When we looked into each other's eyes
We could read minds.
I sit here watching the stars.
Wondering if you remember those times.
When I was the galaxy in your eyes.

Now we're just strangers.
Who daydream about a past life.

A Lesson

The older I get
The harder it is to make excuses.
I'm still not the age you were.
Was it love or lust?
Now, I'm unsure.
At the time, nothing got me higher
Than knowing I was your heroin.
Now, I cringe at the needles I left in your skin.
I take responsibility for the role I played.
And I hope you don't carry the weight
Of the choices I made.
I don't blame you. I don't hate you.
In fact, I wish you well.
I hope you're lying on some beach I can't spell.
The guilt of you I no longer bear.
You're just a lesson,
A badge I no longer wear.

SPRING

Kaleidoscope

You soothed my frostbite.
Gave me a safe place to rest.
An Elysium paradise to clear my head.

Gave me a new perspective.
Allowed me to see colors in a different hue.
Shapes that are intricate and new.
A kaleidoscope of futures unknown.
Healed a side of me, I thought was stone.
Some demons you helped overthrow
With those hazel eyes and charming glow.

Boy Next Door

Shall I compare thee to a spring day?
A gentle breeze making cattails sway.
A gilded sunset compelling birds to sing.
Daffodils and water lilies.

The boy next door,
The rainbow in the sky,
The one who convinced me I could fly.

'Tis the new season!
Color me in mud and scrapes.
We ran through sprinklers,
Where you assured me;
I was more than my mistakes.
Stood up for me when I felt out of place.

Unafraid of my darkness,
You pushed my ghosts aside.
When everyone else shuddered,
You looked me in the eye.

I was too young to realize
Good men are few and far between.
I yelled, cut and fled the scene
Before the best man could get down on one knee.

I was reckless and lost in my head.
What was I to give?
You deserved better,
Not a lifetime of dread.

SPRING

Now, I compare everyone I meet to a spring day.
And they all pale in comparison
To the one that got away.

Homesick

When I think of home,
I think of your lips,
Listening to Death Cab for Cutie
And singing Taylor Swift.

I still can't dance
But I miss your laugh.
Cuddling under the stars,
And coffee with half and half.

Your handwritten notes
And foreign chocolates.
Dirty blonde hair
And coins in your pockets.

Birthday in March.
Of course, you're my Spring.
If I could go back,
I'd give anything.

To feel your body,
To feel your kiss.
Do you remember
My olive dress?

I left my legs bare.
You hadn't noticed,
Too busy matching my stare.
I felt hopeless.

My knees went weak
As the skater boy laid in my sheets.

SPRING

One last kiss
Before, we had to flee.

"Why didn't I go with you?"
I ask all the time.
Now I'm homesick
For a future left behind.

4 AM

Early morning.
We haven't slept.
It's still dark
Which encourages our steps.
Our hearts race because we know
Not to wake the sleeping sparrow.

Everything is black, but I can see
The outline of your hand
Reaching out to me.
The agonizing wait,
Finally, relief
As the gap depletes
And, our hands meet.

I can smell cologne as you pull me in.
My fingers delicate on your bare skin.
Your hair falling in my face.
Your gentle hands around my waist.
I can feel the heat from your chest.
My breath quickens as you tilt my head.
Your lips are just a lick away,
Please, God, let me have a taste.

And that's when I wake
At 4 AM.
All alone
In an empty bed.

Stock The Tea Cabinet

My memory's a bit faded.
Or it's just not how I like to replay it.
So I'll write it new.
Maybe in another dimension, this story is true.
I'll write it for the me that ran away with you.

Your smirk in the morning,
Daffodils glowing,
My playful kisses,
Your soft moaning.

Stock the tea cabinet.
We'll bundle up
In a winter cabin,
Just the two of us.

Play cards next to a fire.
Roll my eyes as you let me win.
Blame it on the rum chocolates
And the white Riesling.

Your diamond mind
Enchanting my wide eyes.
Weak from my name on your lips,
Butterflies as your hands move to my hips.
It's 4 AM
And we haven't slept.

My smirk in the morning,
Water lilies glowing,
Your playful kisses,
My soft moaning.

I'll take Spring in winter.
Can we have Spring in fall?
Spring's the new summer, after all.

Spring

Spring reminds me of you.
Those sunset eyes and Levi jeans.
Running around playing frisbee.
My wandering hands and your soft kisses.
Orange clouds and shooting star wishes.
Lying in a hammock, my head on your chest.
Talking on and on about nonsense.
Laughing, joking, and listening to the beat.
Your wild heart is my favorite melody.
You looked at me fondly and spoke so sweet.
I regret never telling you what you meant to me.
Maybe I was a footnote, but you were a chapter.
I wish I could relive even an hour.
I wonder now if my name has gone sour.
We may be worlds apart
But a piece of you always remains in my heart.

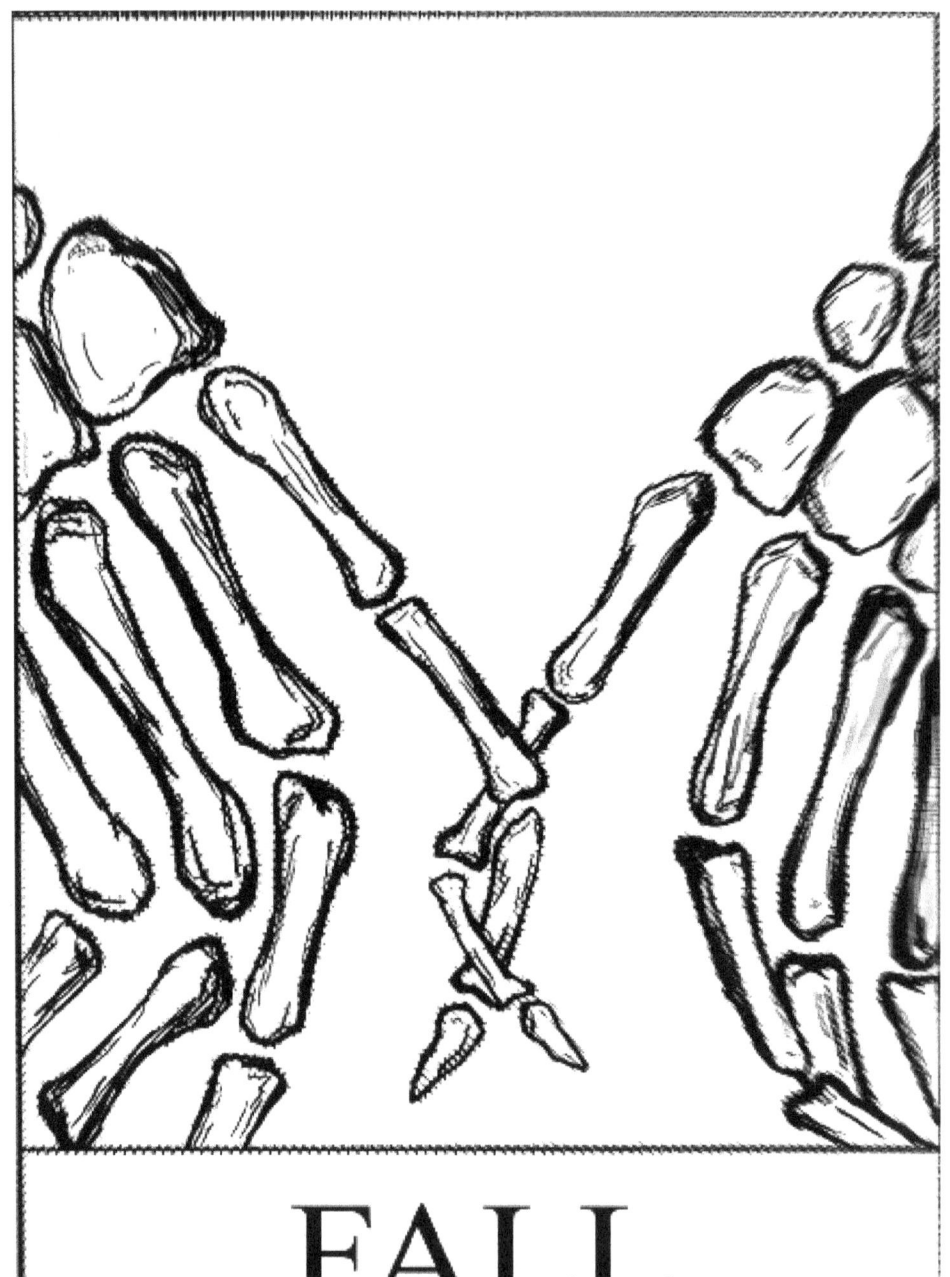

FALL

The Kiss

A small-town cafe
With dusty books.
Tall, dark and handsome,
Laughing in reading nooks.

Sharing secrets,
Sharing tastes,
Subtle glances,
Our friends, misplaced.

They say we're too young.
They say you're trouble,
That I'm crazed,
That we'll stumble
If we misbehave.

What are misfits
Without rules to break?
Heaven and hell couldn't keep us away.

Dreams shared.
Promises made.
Puppy love
And playful games.

You're my safe haven.
My great escape.
In your arms
An endless adventure awaits.

From mountains and road trips
To underground caves.

FALL

The memories of these, I am forever enslaved.
But the one I love most
Is the kiss we exchanged
Inside a bookstore
Above a small-town cafe.

Black Sheep

A city boy from Phoenix
And a small-town girl.
Confined to a box.
Confined to a shell.
They told us to be careful,
So we ran like hell.

Towards a bigger dream
In a bigger world.
Two black sheep
Into the unknown, hurled.

Trails unlearned.
Our future awaits.
A lifetime of laughter
Exploring the states.

Ed Sheeran plays
Down Route 66.
These are the golden days
Submerged in a lavender haze.

Turn the music loud.
We ran from the crowd.
Lost on our own
But we'll figure it out.

Eternal Sun

We're a steady burn.
You're my forever home.
A safety I've never known.
A mosaic of cicatrized souls.
We've come together to be one.
My chosen family.
My eternal sun.

You hold me, and I don't feel alone.
My heart doesn't feel so cold.
Filled my hollow chest with burning coals.
With you, I'll grow old.

Hollow Love

There's an echo in my bones.
You're the hollow love back home.
You're familiar in that way.
You keep asking me to stay.

Don't say those words out loud.
Let's ignore the laughing crowd.
I don't want to be alone.
You're stable enough to hold.

The demons in my cage,
They never go away.
But their screams turn to whispers
Every time you say my name.

Don't say those words out loud.
Let's ignore the barking hound.
I don't want to be alone.
You're stable enough to hold.

You keep me held at night.
For a while, I close my eyes.
A moment of rest
Before I leave the nest.
I wonder if you sense my wickedness.

You know how to read a room,
You keep the storm at bay,
And silent you did stay
You're foreign in that way.

FALL

I feel it in my heart the words you didn't say.
So I speak antonyms and look away.
Can't watch your eyes rain a million enemies.
I'm a villain with no name.
How could words express a sinking ship's pain?

Trusted the ocean to see it through.
Never thought I'd turn my back on you.
But from the start, you should've known.
There was an echo in my bones.
A hollow heart of stone.
You shouldn't commit to a broken home.

Out of Place

I slept next to you and didn't feel safe.
In my home, I felt out of place.

Broken promises.
Broken trust.

The desert heat is not enough to warm your cold touch.
Don't make sacred vows when it's just lust.
But we needed each other like a crutch.
Death by a thousand cuts.

This lake is freezing over,
I can't escape.
Love is not enough.
Breathe deeply if I must
To free us both from Tartarus.

Against The Grain

I've become cold.
I know what's to come.
My heart sinks.
My throat aches.
I think I should run.
But my soul has left my body.
It lingers in the air.
Clings to the silence.
I finally take a breath.
How long have I been holding it in?

I can't move.
And truthfully, I don't want to.
Because as soon as I take a step
Life will demand change.
And I'm not sure I'm brave enough to pave a new way.
Breathing is like going against the grain.
How can something necessary cause so much pain?

Making plans without you is like forgetting something
At the forefront of my brain.
So I close my eyes
And pretend I don't feel a thing.
I tell myself you're bad for me
To help me through this goodbye scene.

Roots In Concrete

I can't write about you.
Can't think about you.
I drive away
Knowing we're through.
I don't look in the mirror.
Need more time to prepare.
Can't accept what's real.
This feels like a nightmare.

Six years, and I draw a blank.
I refuse to acknowledge the weight.
I need to get farther away.
Can't look at the pieces you gave.
Like roots in concrete, you're ingrained.
My throat burns, and my heart aches.
I know I'm losing a best friend.
This isn't how fairytales are supposed to end.

If you were a ghost my body was the host.
Two hearts beating as one.
Maple eyes that felt like embers on the run.
Just two kids trying to have fun.
But it's now fall, and clouds have overcome.

Missing String

I lost your hoodie.
It was a shock to my system.
We had already said goodbye
And I was a thousand miles from home.
But I stole your black one.
The one with the holes and the missing string.
It still smelled like you
And reminded me of our history.

I slept with it
And swore to keep it close.
But when I woke, it was gone.
I tore apart the room
But there was nothing more I could do
And I wondered if that's how you felt, too.

3 Minutes

My mom said don't overthink it.
It's honestly exactly what I needed to hear.
Even so, I couldn't sleep, and I woke up early.

I went for a run that was more of a walk.
I wasn't sad, but I felt like I should be.
I had never gone to court before.
I didn't know what to expect.
I had to sign one last document to finalize the end.
Finalize the death of an oath.
The break of a sacred promise.
We built a mosaic with all our broken pieces,
And today, we smashed it with a hammer.
Or a pen, rather.
I wonder if God turned his head when the ink bled.

It took 3 minutes between printing, signing, returning,
And it was done.
It wasn't slow-motion like the movies,
At least not for me.
There was no hesitation. It was quick.
Almost without a thought.

Everything happened so fast.
The beginning, the middle, the end.
It's as if I am in an entirely new script now.

The marriage ended the same way it began,
Swiftly and with little regard.

FALL

The slow motion happened after.
When I was at the grocery store.
The colors were different.
The fruit not as ripe.
Everything was black and white.
I moved slower.
I wasn't rushing like normal.
I had nowhere to be
And I guess I just liked the company.

Then, it was quiet
And the wave finally fell.
The crash finally came.
I realized the judge called me by *my name.*

I thought about your family.
Your dad especially.
He was always so kind to me.
I thought about how the future is now a mystery.
How our love is a pirate's fantasy.
Just buried treasure lost in history.
Did it ever exist?
Our documents speak differently.
But was it ever really love if it ended in misery?

I chose to believe we indeed had something.
And even just for a second, maybe *everything.*

Sometimes things just happen,
And sometimes things just end.

I wonder if that's how God feels about his creation.

FALL

He loves us, but he just can't stand us.
Cares for us but can't hold our hand.
He divorced us.
For being too much.
Too stubborn, too gay,
Too creative in all the wrong ways.
Too human.

Or maybe there is no God.
And we are just something that happened.
And someday, we will just be something that ends.

Redwood

You hit me in waves.
I slowly allow myself to remember.
I have to take it steady
Or the impact would kill me.

I saw a picture of our house and cried.
I thought I knew what guilt was
Until I read the poem you wrote me
As I got farther from home.

Breaking your heart
Is a pain I've never known.

I know you didn't sleep.
But I couldn't look at your face
Or else I would've stayed.
That house wasn't big enough for my ego
And your games.

They say you can't grow without pain.
Our growth must be the size of a redwood by now.
I feel so old without you around.

Undone

It was so quiet.
The way we parted.
It's as if I snuck out while you slept.
I couldn't finish what we started.
But I think you were awake,
I think you wanted me to escape.
Why else would you allow me
To get so far away?

There was an unspoken break
Before the split in the lake.
Our ties came undone.
We drifted so far.
Parallel lines miles apart.

I don't regret leaving,
But my heart is bleeding.
I still feel the tear
Of the bond we once shared.
In two weeks, it would be our anniversary,
And I can't listen to Noah Kahan
Without thinking of you.
My lungs burn, and my voice shakes,
But I sing anyway.

Tears fall
As I force myself to recall the day we met.
This is me trying
To let new concrete set.

Slowly Let Go

A woman at work asked me about divorce.
She's going through what we went through.
I told her to stick to her guns and take it day by day.
I told her she'd be okay.

I didn't tell her I mourn you twice a year.
I didn't tell her I wish I had a piece of you.
And I didn't tell her in a way; I still do.

I didn't tell her
Because I hope she won't know.
How it feels to slowly let go.

I hope it's quick.
I hope she forgets,
The beginning, the middle, the end.

I hope she didn't lose a best friend.
The way that I did.

Fall

You remind me of fall.
Dark, somber trees,
Book stores in Wisconsin,
And roads too foggy to see.

A warm blanket to hold,
Hot cocoa that cuts the cold,
Maple eyes that were once all on me.
Felt like warm embers being tossed in the sea.
Steam, melting bad dreams.
Or at least masking old memories.

Then came a sobering chill down my spine.
I realized I was naked in a forest of lies.
We're skeletons pretending to be alive.
Lying in a grave, I begged for sunlight,
But you found more comfort in the night.
Where you're able to sleep is where I go to die.

My tombstone tilted.
All my petals had wilted.
You put them between pages
And said, *I love all your stages.*

We were consumed to the point of drowning.
All our leaves were browning.
Can't stay in a lake that's freezing over,
This type of cold is early for October.
We both know you would have endured forever.
And I'd be lying if I said I didn't miss
The comfort of your sweater.

But I'm glad we both found shelter.

Dusty wings

I'm the hollow love back home.
I'm the aching in your bones.
I'm a poison in your veins.
A tremor in your chest that you can't shake.
A bat disguised as a dove.
Manipulation disguised as love.
I'm a goddamn liar
Trapped in a fantasy.
I swear I don't mean to be.

My wings are dusty.
My halo, rusty.
My love doesn't mean a thing.
I don't even know what that word means.
All I know is you deserved better than a beast like me.

THE LIAR

Peace

You were gentle,
Silly and free.
You were at peace.

I was the chaos that brought you to your knee.
Forced your hand, then slapped your face.
You deserved better than my blaze.

You were the ship in my ocean that I kept tipping.
Yet, held me when I thought I was slipping.

I called you cold,
But it's me who is stone.
I speak of love and talk of passion,
But I'm terrified I could never be vulnerable in practice.

You tried to fight,
But I built walls.
You tried to climb,
But I set fires.
We made promises,
But I'm a liar.

I ran away
And you never called.

I hope you find the peace you had
Before I dragged you to the badlands.

SUMMER

Summer Rain

He wasn't the eye of the storm.
He was the calm in the wind after the storm passed.
He was the rain I danced in.

He was fireworks after the war.
A dream like never before.

Dark Honey

You look like heaven and hell.
The beauty of heaven
With a splash of gold.
The seduction of hell,
All consuming, tender,
And a darkness to behold.

Your secrets are of the highest temptation.
I thank a god I don't believe in
For blessing me with your creation.

I see your flames and taste the gin.
With your hand around my neck,
You're my deadly sin.
Have I ever seen such a piercing stare?
Adonis, my love, give me an heir.

Dark honey eyes and the body of a god.
Back sculpted from marble.
Your tongue is something I marvel.

What day is it, my dear?
The tide has finally died.
Breathless and satisfied.
I wonder if you're where my future lies.

Winter who? Fall where?
I have no past.
You've cleansed my palate.

A man with so much talent.

The One That I Miss

I just wanna lay in bed all day.
I just wanna hear you say my name.
I don't think this will last forever
But when I brush some hair from your face
It feels like we're between time and space.

I could stare at you all day.
Are you the one they call Adonis?
Are you going to be the one that I miss?
There isn't a part of you I wouldn't kiss.

How can I describe what it's like to feel your lips?
A crash over my body.
A weakness in my knees.
An ache in my chest, only you can ease.
A fluttering inside.
Chemicals that make me lose my mind.
I think I've gone insane.
The scent on your neck is to blame.

I know all good things come to an end,
But let's stop time for a moment.
Throw the hourglass into the ocean.
Say my name again.
I know love is a feeble notion,
So, let's pretend this is more than lustful emotions.

Grab my hands.
Grab my waist.
Grab every part of me.
I'm yours to take.

SUMMER

Tell me all the different ways I can make you shake.
Just stay in bed with me today.

Let me explore your mind. Let me kiss your scars
And tell you how divine I think you are.

We don't have much time,
But when I look into your eyes, I feel infinite.
I feel alive.

Please stay here. All day
And all night.

A Perfect Day

Cold water,
Chattering teeth,
A perfect day,
A million muscles relieved.

You watched me swim.
Told me how beautiful I am.
Held me as I shivered.
Savory warmth, your body delivered.

Naming turtles
And walking upstream.
Your broad shoulders.
My heart screaming.

Pink waves crashed the sky
As you drove me home.
We ate key lime pie
And got stoned.

You brushed the hair from my face
And kissed my freckles.
I caressed your arm
As I told you about my goals.

You sang along to The Killers.
I showed you, Phoebe Bridgers.

A perfect end to a perfect day.
I will always remember us this way.

Favorite Hymn

Our souls entangled like salt in the sea.
When you breathe, I breathe.
When you dance, I sway.
Look in my eyes
Here as we lay.
This is what poets die for
And what the rest of the people strive for.

I pray to your altar.
You're my favorite hymn.
Only for you would I not sin.

This angel worships your crown.
Your golden eyes and my silver stare.
I could live here forever in this Empyrean lair.

Holy Land

You're tight-lipped,
But it's not your fault.
Your shield is up from the last battle.
I can see the spear in your back.
You left it there from the last attack.
And I am just a quick stitch patch.

I'll bring you ice and hold your hand.
You may feel like hell.
But to me, you're holy land.

I miss you, and I don't know why.
You're still mine for the rest of the night.
I guess I can tell you're in mid-flight.
Her claws dug deep
And I'm not fit for fight.
I've only got love, and it's yours tonight.
I've only got love, and it's yours for life.

Summer

You remind me of summer.
Yellow flowers,
A sunrise on the bluff,
A warm, sultry sun
That never seems to last long enough.

Our time, cut short in the blink of an eye.
My favorite time of the year
Has passed me by.
Why did Winter feel so long?
Fall was an eternity.
But Summer slipped through my fingers.
Your old t-shirt is all that lingers.

I'm chasing memories like trying to catch the wind.
You're my joie de vivre, not my deadly sin.
How I miss the way your sun shines on my skin.

I wish I could run back in time,
Pause every moment,
Savor every second.
I swear I tried while the moment was prime.
Adonis, my love, you are one of a kind.

A sliver of hope in dark honey eyes.
You're a beacon of light in clouded skies.
A piece of my heart is yours for life.

Of all our promises, I hope the one you keep
Is the one where you promised to thrive.

SUMMER

My darling Summer, you've healed my soul.
I hope you find your Summer,
Wherever you go.

All Over Again

Your brows were furrowed all night.
We knew this would be the last time.
You said, "Baby, stay close."
As we tried to make the most.
I prayed to time she'd be kind and patient.
But the hours she promised
Were mere minutes, mere seconds. I hate her.
And I'm angry with you.
How dare you be so beautiful. How dare you be so sweet.
How dare you do this to me.

I tear myself apart and run away
But I never get too far before I start to see your face.
In the wind,
In the rain,
When the sun shines on my skin,
I know I'd do it all over again.

White Lie

You said you missed your old life.
I guess I appreciate the honesty.
I'm sure, at one point, she was lovely.
But is she not a mirage of misplaced memory?

I almost wish you'd get back with her
Just so you can see, it's not as good as you remember.
You're Summer stuck in December.
And I was July begging for your light.
I know what it's like to have a past life.

I was ready to start from scratch.
For you, that was a daunting task.
But I don't blame you.
You were still catching your breath
When I was ready to dive in.
I fear I'm your Spring.
And one day you'll regret me leaving.

I tried to tell you you were the sun.
You said you didn't feel like enough.
What I think you meant to say is, you wouldn't try.
So, I accepted your white lie as a goodbye.

SUMMER FLING

Summer Fling

It was love at first sight for me.
But I was a blur among the faceless.
Your day would've been all the same
Whether or not we had exchanged names.

I called you Adonis.
You called me cute.
I called you beautiful.
You called me sweet.
I said I adore you.
And you fell asleep.

I romanticized a house
And four little feet.
I got lost in your eyes
And melted in your kiss.
I craved every touch
And knew you'd be the one that I'd miss.
You were my Adonis.   .

I wanted to be your Aphrodite.
Not just some girl you happened to meet.
You were so special to me.
I was just a summer fling.

You were my Summer
And I was just another girl in Raleigh.

Would Have

We never said it.
I thought it was more romantic
That we said it in every other way
Except with our voices.
But I would have screamed it.

I wanted to shout it at the river.
I wanted to whisper it during our picnic.
And in the morning
I wanted to mumble it through soft kisses.

But I knew I wouldn't hear it back.
And I don't think my ears could have handled
A tragedy like that.

I didn't dig myself out of a grave,
Raise my sails and ride the waves,
Only to be with someone too afraid.

Fallen Angel

My outstretched hand,
Your nose to the sky,
I fell from the clouds.
My hopes were so high.

I'm a fallen angel.
You ignored my cries.
You're not where my future lies.

Your kingdom's beyond my reach.
Forgive my blasphemy,
But you abandoned me.

Gentle Lover

You were so calm.
A relief after so much running.
I had never been cared for
The way you cared for me.
Wounds that I couldn't even see.

I know how much I meant to you.
We healed each other
And I loved being your gentle lover.
I'm sorry I got bitter.
You will always be my Summer.

THE SKELETON

The Skeleton

I almost wish I stayed.
Not because I regret leaving,
But because you loved me so fiercely.
For that, I am sorry.
Not for you,
But for me.
I think I could've learned something.
I couldn't accept you on your knees,
I can only love what's beyond my reach.

I have been loved so deeply and so beautifully.
A superpower I lack.
Why could I never reciprocate that?

I beg for love,
Say, I'd die for passion.
I want to be The Lover.
But the truth is,
I'm The Dreamer.
I'm The Runner.
I'm The Liar.

As soon as three words are said,
As soon as I'm truly convinced,
I realize I'm incapable of it.
All the things I write about.
All the things I cried over.
I'm a wolf in sheepskin.
A heartless skeleton.

So no, I don't feel sorry for you.

THE SKELETON

I feel sorry for me.
All I want to do is bleed,
And bleed,
And bleed,
And bleed.

I call myself a hopeless romantic.
A love fanatic.
Still, keep all your pictures in my attic.
That the bonds we shared would never be undone.

But the truth is,
I'm just a dead skeleton
Who writes poems for fun.

THE LOVER

THE SUN

Solitude

I kept running towards something.
I couldn't name.
In the stars, I see her face.
I finally meet my eyes.
I'm not afraid of my reflection.
I finally took the time.
To learn what was inside.

Everything I've ever needed
I already own.
Solitude doesn't mean alone.
I love you
Doesn't mean home.
True friendship is true love.
I no longer feel like a crow
But a dove.

Being best friends with yourself is a must.
I kept asking why I wasn't enough.
Never learned to love the woman in the glass.
Never imagined I could remove the mask.
Afraid to show you what was underneath.
But I realized the only approval I need
Is from me.

My feet don't feel so uncertain.
My heart doesn't feel like a burden.
Being without you doesn't feel like desertion.

I looked for pieces of me
In all of you.

THE SUN

But now I'm free.
My noose has been undone.
I know that I am the sun.

Film Credits

The truth is
You were a dream.
I cherish you and I always will.
I'm grateful for the love. I'm grateful for the pain.
I've grown fond of the ghosts that haunt me
And I now dance when they say your name.

I needed you as proof I wasn't cursed.
That I actually had worth.
Desperate for affection I wasn't shown.
Finding love in your arms instead of finding it in my own.

I'll take back my heart from the moon.
The sun will give me my skin.
I'm a recovering skeleton.

I begged for sleep to fall in reverie.
But it's time to wake up.
It's time to let go.
You helped me heal.
You helped me grow.

Let the film credits roll.

Was I Your Muse?

Was I the love of your life?
Was I the girl next door?
Was I everything you wanted and more?
Was I the fairytale dream?
The eye of the storm?
Was I the one that got away?
Am I who you see when you watch porn?

Do you think of me often?
Do I cause fights?
Am I the insidious thought that keeps you up at night?
Was I the devil knocking at your door?
A nightmare like never before?
Salt in a wound?
Oil to a flame?
A chaos that can't be tamed?

Was I death by a thousand cuts?
A demon to be slayed?
Or did you think of me as just a pawn in a game?
A random number?
Thoughtless act of lust?
Have all our memories turned to rust?

I wish you'd tell me.
I want the truth.
Did I make you bleed?
Was I your muse?
Or was I nothing more
Than a 30-second prelude?

Happy Ending

The words I scream in my head but don't say out loud.
Is it all worth it in the end not to make fools of ourselves?

Should I be the clown and speak my mind?
Watch the people cringe at my lines.
Would it be worth it once they see me fly?
Only to fall at the end of my time?

If I dance under the stars and sing to the sun,
Pick wildflowers to share with loved ones,
Scream to the mountains, "I love you more."
Sit around a fire and tell folklore.
If I jump in the water and run in the mud,
Talk to the trees and tell secrets to grubs.
I promise to share with you all that I know.
Will it all be worth it when I'm six feet below?

All my love and all my kisses,
My subtle glares and earnest wishes.
The rush I get when touching your skin,
Electric skies and soft linen.
My hands in your hair and yours on my thigh.
Can we please stop time and enjoy the high?
All this passion would make them envy.
This moment with you will soon be a memory.
I'd bottle it up and store it like fine whiskey
But alas, I am human.
I can't take my brain with me.
Will it all be worth it when I'm nothing but history?

THE SUN

Love under the moon and play in the ocean.
An adventure with me that might leave you broken.

Would you shake your head at this mistake?
Would my love be a waste if it ends with heartache?
Would you start something knowing there's no mending?
Is it all worth it, even if there's no happy ending?

Authors Note

Thank you for reading Reverie. The entirety is not about suicide but it was mentioned so I feel compelled to speak on it briefly. I also wish to clarify that no one has ever influenced my decision to end my life. I take full responsibility for my actions. I was motivated by self hatred which led me to make choices that would push me closer to the edge. If you have ever felt that way too, please take immediate action to ask for help. You are not a burden. You are not alone. One of the biggest changes I had to make was how I spoke to myself inside my head. I would encourage you to do the same. Your thoughts are so powerful. Thoughts become actions. Think kind to yourself. Act kind to yourself. Keep going.

Something I failed to realize was the pain I felt inside wouldn't go away if I died; it would simply be transferred to all the people who loved me the most. Whom I love the most.

Never underestimate the aching hole you would leave in the world's collective chest if something happened to you. The family member, classmate, friend of a friend, or even the stranger that passed by you and thought to themselves how lovely you are. After all, don't stories about complete strangers' suicides make your heart ache?

The residue of your absence would be significant, devastating, never-ending.

You have yet to meet all the people who will love you. I dare you to find them. Dare you to try something new. Dare you to find yourself. Dare you to love yourself. I dare you tomorrow.

www.ingramcontent.com/pod-product-compliance
Lightning Source LLC
Chambersburg PA
CBHW051548120626
46551CB00013B/1423